# Tide Tables

# Tide Tables

Poems by

Nancy Anne Miller

Cover art by Nancy Anne Miller
Cover design by Shay Culligan

ISBN: 978-1-950462-30-8

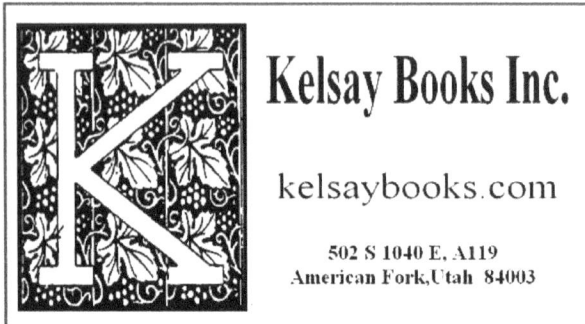

Kelsay Books Inc.

kelsaybooks.com

502 S 1040 E, A119
American Fork, Utah 84003

*for Arthur Franklin Miller Jr.*

Nothing of him that doth fade
But doth suffer a sea-change
Into something rich and strange.
—*The Tempest*

And in me too, the wave rises.
      —Virginia Woolf, *The Waves*

# Introduction

Poets teach us that there is something More, the invisible "deeper in" than the surface, but that we only get to it through the immediate, the concrete. A certain haunting by the ever-present "more" is a common experience. Becket wrote "[In] the identification of immediate with past experience...what is common to present and past is more essential than either taken separately...the ideal real, the essential, the extratemporal."

There are many ways into this extratemporal—and extra spatial-reality. Metaphor can get us there. It sets up a field between poles and invites us to enter and go deeper, there in the resonance. Nancy Anne Miller is a master here—brilliant metaphors peal out like bells along our walk among her poems. Good metaphors, though they are so much more, can be fun. When she writes of the now-stripped late fall trees with the leaves scattered around beneath them as "days of uncollected mail on the porch" that, whatever else it is, is just so... neat! We laugh. But often enough the fun simply dissolves into pure loveliness as in the breathtaking lines about the lighthouse girl, "she raises her skirt like a folded sail as she ascends the conch spiraled staircase" Here as in the "the silver urn for tea placed ritualistically on the linen tablecloth as if an altar" we approach the Holy. And the sea of Miller's beloved Bermuda shimmers and crashes everywhere in these poems, yes, at the lighthouse, but also in the April woods where in the forsythia branches "spring fights winter back, like pirates fought over a bobbing ship's domain in a clamorous sea"

These poems are continuously recollective: "I was civilized here" and so, harking Beckett, we get yet another dimension. And that is it—in an age of insistent one-dimensionality Miller helps us live in more than one, which is where we belong. Give thanks for this testimony of gentle and canny joy.

Roger Duncan, Resident Philosopher,
The Promisek Community, Bridgewater, CT

# Acknowledgments

*I would like to thank the editors of the following journals for publishing my works.*

*The Caribbean Writer (VI):* "Every Civilization," "Postal," "St. Valentine's Prayer," "Tide Tables"

*Dodging the Rain (IE):* "England Taught Me," "Anne vs Ann," "To Keep the Light," "Because You Were Taught to Look," "Back Scrubber"

*Moko(TT):* "Welcoming in the New Legal Year 2018"

*Poetry Ireland Review(IE):* "Mosquito Net at Elma Napier's Estate"

*Poetshead (IE):* "I was Raised in Houses," "Scarab Bracelet," "Postal Mark," "Emerald Cross," "St. Valentine's Prayer"

*Poetry Pacific(CA):* "Walker," "April Fools,"

*Poetry South (USA):* "Halter," "Tide Tables"

*Postcolonial Text (CA):* "The Geography of Tea," "Plastic Ocean," "Oration," "Not the Country I Was Born In," "Fly Away," "Global"

*The Taj Mahal Review (IN):* "Ruling Bodies"

*The Country and Abroad (USA)*: "Too Many Angels,""Jesus of the Highways," "Body Language," "Home Front," "Map-Less," "Day after Valentines"

# Contents

Learning Not to Be Busy

Cane Frogs                                              19
Learning Not to be Busy                                 20
Un-Heard                                                21
Opening Up the Legal Year 2018                          22
Cruising through Bermuda's Cliques                       23
Catch as Catch Can                                      24
We, Still                                               25
To Keep the Light                                       26
St. Valentine's Prayer                                  27
I Was Raised in Houses                                  28
Love Letter                                             29
Lolli Pop                                               30
Corsage                                                 31
I Lika da Shoes                                         32
Scarab Bracelet                                         33
Solitaire                                               34
Geography Lesson                                        35
Discovering the Sea Venture                             36
A Cut Above                                             37
Emerald Cross                                           38
Sea Hunger                                              39
Man Overboard                                           40
Easter Rising                                           41

The Geography of Tea

Postal                                                  45
No Need                                                 46
Global                                                  47
The Geography of Tea                                    48
Fly Away                                                49
Mosquito Net at Elma Napier's Estate                    50

Anne vs Ann                                51
Plastic Ocean                              52
Carry On                                   53
Full                                       54
Every Civilization                         55
England Taught Me                          56
Memorial                                   57
Home Front                                 58
Wish Bone                                  59
Ruling Bodies                              60
Oration                                    61
A Note                                     62
Because You Were Taught to Look            63
Poldark                                    64
Not the Country I Was Born In              65

Tide Tables

Tide Tables                                69
Halter                                     71
Walker                                     72
Long Gaited                                73
Not Even Here                              74
Jackets Hung                               75
Wag                                        76
Heart Worm                                 77
Bark                                       78
House Broken                               79
Crackers                                   80
Dogs with Tumours                          81
Body Language                              82
Map-Less                                   83
Jesus of the Highways                      84
Back Scrubber                              85

The Sun's Strobe

Bone China                        89
Too Many Angels                   90
The Sun's Strobe                  91
Sealed Silence                    92
Liposuction                       93
First Christmas Card              94
Wreath                            95
Relief                            96
Dead Head                         97
Fistfuls                          98
How to End Winter                 99
Clean Up                         100
Day After Valentines             101
Spring Rising                    102
April Fools                      103

Learning Not to Be Busy

# Cane Frogs

My hands veined, spotted
like island cane frogs

hopping across Ord Road
in the bliss of rain. One stops

in the middle, stares into
my Mobylette's headlight,

a Buddha in a temple lined
with curtains of silvery satin.

Legs unfold like pantyhose
pulled from a L'eggs container

before Spanx. Another hit, a glue
like venom emits from the body,

expands into an open passenger
airbag, then flattens into wings

of a tubby cherub. Outspread
ligaments secured to the pavement's

grievous grey, a bumpy medieval
gargoyle on a French cathedral.

# Learning Not to be Busy

*De heat has got me.*
    —May DeSilva


Is what I learned growing
up in Bermuda. The waves
up, down, tilt rocked me
into a sunny sleep/walking/ness.

To be awake but feel my
body slip through the black
keyhole of my shadow. As if
dreaming is the way to open

the lock of the semitropical
landscape where whispery
accents of Bermudians, the down
beat hush tone, is a lullaby

in light. My shadow's over-
night bag bunches near when
I sit, so I find what I need
to nod off. Like night clothes,

a dancing doll attaches to my
feet, steps whichever way I
move into heat hot days,
hushes me towards a time to rest.

# Un-Heard

*The Queen's English is a dialect.*
                              —Kei Miller

It is always at the airport, JFK,
Bermudian voices call me back,
before airborne. Sound waves
rise over steel toothed seats,
levies break, rush words, a hot
sun shadows. An undertow, I
gladly swim, float tropical currents
un-heard in the Northeast.

The past present future start up,
a terminal floor escalator,
rushes me home. I shaped my
landscape in a setting accent,
pitched the world in sloping
degrees, down shifted into tone's
dark angle where humidity makes
language barely breathe. *De vurds*

*flow dawn de sides to de mouf,*
*sveet and loquat stained.* Joined
me with black, white, coloured,
maid, groom, and gardener about.
Push peddle verbs, and melting
subjects, traveled me out from
the Queen's English, a young
Bermewjun to the land she claimed.

# Opening Up the Legal Year 2018

The wigs take the law into the feminine,
men and women long-haired.

As if a bit of surf got attached
to their forehead, skull, rhythms of

South Shore guide them as
they sit in cedar partitions like

levies the ocean might crash
through. Okay, we all know the sea

is the subconscious, so here it is
symbolized in the new legal year,

keeping up habits of the old. I
think they all look like their locks

are still in rollers, haven't gotten
quite awake enough yet to work.

Still sea rocked by the maritime deep,
lulled by the hushes of a mother soothing.

# Cruising through Bermuda's Cliques

It was a young boy's lost cricket ball,
a sun wanting to cool, fell down a hole
into crystal caves where frozen clouds
sagged rain, like old hose on a line.

It was too many hogs squealing
delight, had the run of the place,
gave the name *isle of devils,*
a wicked joke on the greedy when

one adorned a penny. It was men
at work, cut linen trousers to thwart
heat, legs, knitting needles above
woolen socks. It was dark, stormy

nights at sea, made a sailor empty
a rum bottle to slip a ship in. It was
surreys on taxis, a sun umbrella held,
that made tourists Victorian royalty.

# Catch as Catch Can

The angle of snow evokes:
*Tell it slant!* The curve of
the palm tree leaf as it drizzles
water from rain. Beads bounce

down undulating waves of
a whitewashed roof, to shoot
through the lower gutter.
Reminiscent of a game of

getting the orange plastic
ball through the maze I bought
at Paget Pharmacy when
bored. Like a Skittles one shot

to sink in the corner hole, aimed
through wooden figures, standing
like cricket players on a village
green about to be bowled over.

When did this catch as catch
can game start? An African
Bermudian sitting next to me
on my flight home to BDA

said in Sandy's they snatched
singers off the casuarinas,
put them in match boxes, to
hold to ears, to hear wings hum.

# We, Still

We still do this, recite
our ancestry, locate ourselves,
the other, as we sit here on
Longtail Terrace in rocking
chairs, sip afternoon tea.

Such a small space to claim,
make the odds great. Like
Gombeys re-owning the streets
in vivid colour, rhythms from
a hidden history, now known.

In a game of lawn tennis, we
waft names back, forth, thread
the eye of a racket's needle to
stitch our mutual belonging,
strain blood lines through its

spoon shaped net. Cousins found,
sir names like rain go down deep, in
old Tribe Roads to water roots.
The tide in, out to sea, wants to suck
us away, each wave pushes us back
to where a rogue storm planted us.

# To Keep the Light

She raises her skirt
like a folded sail
as she ascends the
conch spiraled staircase,
full of the sky's
dizzy whisperings.

The flame of the large
lamp, a needle's eye in
the rags of the clouds
she watches. A sea captain,
to see what a storm brings,
full of lightning's stitching.

The spinning steps up,
causes a dervish
trance, the ecstasy of
circling. The latitude,
longitude cut of flashes,
the golden pigtail of a girl twirls.

# St. Valentine's Prayer

*If I forget thee, O Jerusalem, let my right hand forget her cunning.*
—Psalm 137:5

In the February light the tone of
grey hue falls to the ground,
off the maple trees, like shadows
boiled down in a broth, the way

snapper bones collapse into an island
chowder. Midmonth I gravitate
to Valentine's Day for a CPR
exercise, bring the blood back to

my Bermudian heart, feel it flutter
in my ribs, as a red squirrelfish
might in my hand when I
took the hook out of its kissing

lipstick mouth. I was taught
*Love is Blind* Saint Valentine,
but you restore sight to daughters
of a judge, a jailer. Bring back

my semitropical vision, where
I am barred by twiggy woods,
send pleas to the high court sky
arced by ancient oaks strong as

island cedars. Branches scribbly
cataracts, block the heavenly
view where a star might shoot
the dark, one of your curving arrows.

# I Was Raised in Houses

I was raised in houses, welcoming arms
in front, like those of May, my nanny.
Where the end of their stony reach curled back
into the bob of a magistrate's wig, who
executes law in The House of Parliament.

Where the crooked teeth of brick steps
broke into a wide smile on entrance,
mimic my West Indian gardener's. I took pea
soup for lunch, as he sat on the shed stoop, door
parted behind, gapped, like a front molar missing.

I was raised in houses where the lee winds blew
down the chimney top as if the mouth of
a whistle, call us to close shutters before
the storm came. Each one pushed up afterwards,
opening a grave's slab after it blew through.

I was raised in houses where ants trailed
the wet pillars on the porch, like the seam
in silk stockings my mother wore to go
out to dinner. Where ceiling fans spun
North, East, South, West, a compass

needle locating us, seven hundred miles
at sea. Where limestone blocks were cut
from land, a quarry turned into a back
yard garden. Homes resting forever,
look to the rock from whence hewn.

I was raised in houses, roofs team with
white, the tide of South Shore about to take
you under. Caught daily raindrops for the tank
outback, spotted with damp moss, lay
under calm hibiscus, like an overturned punt.

# Love Letter

The postal mark from Perot Post Office,
Queen Street, Hamilton, a sun,
heat waves waver over an Empire.

The wings of a cherub, full of love, news
sent via mail, via correspondence from
my island to America where autumn

trees burn the year's letters by fire.
Postal mark, a mouth trembles with a kiss,
the lipstick bleed of passion blown

across miles where oceans roll like
aerogramme lines. Postal mark, a Bermuda
Land Crab, a shell protects the heart inside.

# Lolli Pop

The large sun umbrellas
on Longtail Terrace, closed,
yellow, tied, lollipops from
France I buy to decorate
my dinner table. Sweet.

The island thus for me.
Oleanders bushes discard
leaves shaped like large minnows,
'fries' in the water along Harbour
Road. Move, form a suspended

nest, like memory quicksilver,
turns. Shifts, a temporary
home. Each wave coming
in on South Shore foam
crested. A hand white

knuckles it, to hold onto
the sea's rhythm, a child
clings to its own clothes,
before the tide breaks
open, reaches, reshapes the shore.

# Corsage

The palm trees lit with Christmas bulbs:
pink, turquoise, orange explode like

fireworks against the humid island sky,
a carnival street welcome on my return

to the isle as the taxi takes me away from
the airport. They line the route out of

the parking lot, horrific as underwater
sponges with spikey torsos, Kitchen Maid

rubber glove fingers sift the sky like water.
More celebratory than the Advent Balsam Fir,

prickly with death's scent. Arced in giving,
the palm drops gifts of fruit throughout

the balmy year. Now is a gigantic corsage
pinned to the isle, for motherhood, for fussing.

# I Lika da Shoes

*I lika da shoes,* the elderly Portuguese woman says to me in
Lindo's market on Middle Road. She is dressed in black, hair
in a bun, a style the elderly Portuguese use to wear on the isle.

My brother asked me at the club: *Are they meant to
correct your feet?* Dansko, Mary Jane sandals, bought
for comfort, support, descendants of clogs, used to scale

mountains in Northern Europe, suit a woman at ease in her life,
whatever the challenge. I tell her she can get them
on the web if she Googles Dansko. She repeats *I lika da shoes.*

*I do too.* I no longer tie toes up in the bow of Capezios
flats like asparagus for dinner. Instead, I allow them to
breathe through holes, wriggle about wormy, seek rich soil.

# Scarab Bracelet

The UPS man says you always have to sign
for Belgian Shoes. I write my name in the grey
plastic slot like a Hollywood actor in wet cement
for the Avenue of Stars. I have arrived.

Black patent leather shiny as a new car,
gondolas for my slightly Italian heritage.
They will help me walk on, float pietistic waters
of old age. What makes a woman retrieve

a scarab bracelet from her jewelry box and wear
it after forty years? Like the dung beetle of Egypt
laying eggs in excrement, I do what I need for
rebirth from what I once so easily eliminated.

# Solitaire

It has become that trivial,
whatever it is the woman
sitting next to her husband
views as they both gaze
into their I phone mirrors.

She may as well say *Shoo!*
like Baroness Blixen on
route to Nairobi, to chase
the natives away that
have interrupted her path.

No train of thought can stand
the fore finger's whims. Pointing
the news of hurricane Florence
trailing Bermuda away, as if to
send her to her room. Is it survival,

as global warming engulfs a planet?
Will we each become stations,
flicking luminous cells, like
shedding what is no longer
needed, dealing cards for solitaire.

# Geography Lesson

The pages are tainted brown, like
the dusty khaki terrain the Malawi
Chief with a towering headdress
stands on in an Empire photo.
The image bleeds light, a flame lily
pressed between covers. The book,

not circular, like learning from
the globe I would spin in my
BHS classroom, Form I, imagine
ships crawling the equator,
white cabbage butterflies on
a dappled sugar melon. Countries

hidden between pages, split open
into the wake of a wave a vessel makes
on a journey, a map on my knees,
like a folding card table where
Mombasa, Nepal, Cairo said aloud
are passports in the air. Unlike Google

Earth, I zoom in, out, get seasick
in the blur, see women herd goats
in Tunisia, a voyeur, not a voyager,
without the locus of syllables,
consonants, alphabet's timbre in my
throat, to sound out lives I can read.

# Discovering the Sea Venture

For certain it stayed above ground
for years like a good matron to make
sure all the passengers brought to this
shore were safe and would prosper.

Then it sank into the passage it slipped
through, laid down in the bed it made,
where divers looked for her like offspring
of the old woman who lived in a shoe.

A Dutch pipe almost gave her her name,
the puff shape of an exhaled breath, made
her identity smoky. A pottery jar from the
West Country scattered in bits turned the sloop

into a mouth of teething, spoke the wreck was
she. So, when dimensions of her hull matched
the geometric shape of nautical booklet # nine,
Bermudians knew, she was the circumference

of their mother's hips the sea pounded
through, like the dropped waters before
a birth, the torrent of waves rushing to shore,
needed to release her children onto an island.

# A Cut Above

*after The American Cup*

It is the hand reeling I can't quite get,
like bringing a fish in from the deep sea,
but this is more manual sewing machine
rotation, strong sailors engaged in dainty work.

But not, because body weight is a ballast,
sails need steering at such tremendous speed,
to stay lifted above water, above the maritime
history of boats pressing into it with a leaf

like shape, memory of trees, the woods
rooted down, tentacles of a Humboldt Squid.
This is a cut above, lifter board, a wrench's
mouth closes the gap between sky, water.

# Emerald Cross

She made the cross with two sticks,
tied the middle like a bow on a package,
the four lines of willow bark, the ribbon on a gift.

Tightly pulled as if to keep the sky's four corners
secure, stable. The North, East, South, West
points un-negotiable for a young poet sitting,

thinking about the Body the far tips were made to
stretch, to fit each part of her life. Later used to
water witch up her subconscious, the ocean's

great undertow, waves like the crest of a hill
she placed it on in CT.  Floated her to the island's
deep where the Emerald Cross was found, jewels,

drops of semitropical water in the locus of the Sargasso.
Latitude, Longitude of the Gulf Stream's roar, crossed
for where, whence poems come, blown in, up from high seas.

# Sea Hunger

*for Nick Hutchings*

*Dey are pulling de bye to de back of de boat,*
like a lure with bait to catch a shipwreck,
big gaping mouth of hull below mimics

the sea's hunger. Ballast rocks strewn,
a boney spine to uncover the craft, step-
ping stones towards the mystery. *Vhat*

*you saw was vhat you got!* Divers
could claim pottery the rocking waves
shattered, uncovered in the sea's filmy

plastic wrap around a site. Now, a tidier
endeavor, artifacts noted, placed behind
glass: a deconstructed sentence without

the ocean's roar to pound in meaning.
Sands shift no matter, *pay no mind,*
a hide and seek game below a reef's

dominion where today a ship is there,
tomorrow isn't while the grain of logs
locate origins, a Mapquest of where a boat

embarked. *A 24 hour diving day is a 72*
*hour one!* says the Keeper of Wrecks,
the journey in the wake of a find, ripples,

shifts time. In BDA some technology
*useless,* volcanic lava disguises, slows
work down, while tanks tick seconds

like bombs. Air bubbles fragile as glass beads
about to break, a toss of silver coinage back
to the depths, every moment a treasure.

# Man Overboard

*for Nathaniel White Hutchings*

Each Day Nathaniel White
Hutchings would walk from
'Lee Winds' down Tribe Road,
before he placed a fresh
carnation in his jacket lapel,
to crown the day.  Each day.

To swim firstly, wrestle
the surf like an ungainly sail
on a schooner an ancestor
could not fold up. Place his back
to the horizon, ride a wave in
after it flowed over his head,

hooded him, a priest in a habit,
belonged him to the sea again.
Where Sargassum floats, like
synapses from the salty blood
of so many ship captains, tided
by the ocean, owning them.

# Easter Rising

We already know their spout
of frilly water flowering above
their backs is a sign of an Easter
rising, as heavy bodies slap

through water like galoshes.
We know too the spray of
a white fountain above a black
grave is resurrection enough,

the spirit leaving the body. But
we are also keen to see a tail above
water: a turnkey for the season,
the wings of a bird flap wide open.

The Geography of Tea

.

# Postal

The tall red royal box, a soldier
at his post for the Queen,
all correspondence put in one by
one by hand, a salute to order,
the thin seriousness of the word, stately
like handwriting taught in school.

America's mail box, a wide
stout mouth to accommodate
everything said by the body it
could also fit in. Freedom of speech
on every home town corner,
wide as an easily opened trash bin.

# No Need

To add fire to the sky, crack it open,
a robin egg blue with zig zags of electric

light. A heat wave unravels, flags the land,
a banner of sparks about to break lightning.

Let the Day Lilies rise instead, burst, be
noticed, lift soft cups up. Earth wants

the smokiness of rain, humid steam of
cooling. We explore roving freedoms,

drive cars with hot mufflers, like flicked
celebratory cigars, choke with fumes.

Daisies curled into the last cusps of June with
a *Loves me? Loves me not?* chant as we tug,

pull a center. The pinwheel of choices we note
today, pluck, pluck petals until a bald sun remains.

# Global

*I use to make those circular thatch bags,*
*when I was a child in Honduras!* the woman says
to me inside the Pantry. A golden cymbal announces
loudly that I too am from a warm country and still

carry this portable sun, I always want near into
colder months. I open its mouth up as she and I peer
into it like a shell forced open for a pearl. The man
in the documentary about the Andes, says all seasons

are becoming one. He believes it is a sign of the end.
The anthropologist filmmaker climbs the mountain
to retrieve a block of ice as dear these days as a diamond.
In Kiribati, the islands she visits become saturated

watercolours, a washout, blur, lose the delicacy
of imagery. Their flag, a sunset above island waves,
mimic rivulets of heat, where a bird is suspended,
no longer able to weave, make a straw nest, land.

# The Geography of Tea

The kettle's high pitch,
a vexing against *all* ills,
the village women's *hiss,*
ward*s* off evil. The shrill

sound of the wind whipping
casuarinas as a hurricane
circles the island. This
bitter brew we savour,

put in sugar, cream, make
sweet. Indian tea pickers, carry
a basket on their back, thrust
leaves over their shoulders in

a reversal of the child's tipsy
game. *I'm a little teapot,*
*small and stout, tip me over*
*and pour me out.* The thick

green bushes grow like pieces
of a puzzled map where
countries try to join. Upstairs
china is fine enough for hot

chai to go in first, won't crack.
Downstairs crockery breaks
without milk first in a cup, like
a doily from the mother country.

# Fly Away

The propeller passenger,
plane over Africa 1943,
looks so heavy, clumsy,

an Oldenburg sculpture
might fall from the sky.
Out of date like 50's

household items. The mixer
with dual spinners, whirls
batter, two birds about

to take off. The peak of
a soufflé, the mountain tip
in Kenya where women defy

gravity, balance papayas, eggs
in a basket on heads, without,
so thin, they might fly away.

# Mosquito Net at Elma Napier's Estate

The mosquito net above the bed,
ghost of a writer who once visited her.

The spirit leaves the body above a caved
in mattress, sunken, about to collapse.

So many fictions dreamt on it. The muslin
ties at the bottom, like a mango heavy in

a string market bag she bought in Baptiste.
Hangs like an exclamation mark for

the filmy subconscious more vivid than
the mountain view outside the window.

And more present than the mosquitos
gathering on its airy white slopes at night.

# Anne vs Ann

Lopped off by some
Caribbean editors, the *e*
evokes the name of
a British Queen whose

presence adorned
furniture, stiffens one
with extra backbone,
gives one lion's feet to

sit in the Empire's roar.
Without the e, *common,*
as if shortened from bananas
amply found on a Tribe Road.

Multi-fruit hang, clustered,
a flock of canaries homed. In
the market, tips of a gaggle
splay into the British sunrise.

# Plastic Ocean

I unravel a wave of plastic,
to cover the cheese plate,
clear as water at Ely's Harbour,
see through to view a soft brie,
like a soggy sifting sandbar. This

surge of Saran Wrap will flow
all the way to the ocean where
the slit stomach of the swordfish
has bits of pink, orange, yellow
in its esophagus, mimics a mosaic

coffee table. Dolphins dive in
curves like a can opener cutting
the rim of a steely sea. The ocean
has a smog, a net hangs from
the surface, catches our attention.

A cruel joke about how a butterfly's
fluttering wing in Japan affects
me. I throw away my Pellegrino
water bottle, a disposable bomb,
blows apart in an in-disposable ocean.

Reefs, seaweed, fish absorb broken
pieces, float back to me
in the coral coloured meat
of a salmon, I believe I am
eating to be in the pink of health.

# Carry On

The Samsonite Carry On Luggage
looks like a bullet vest, the crisscross straps
inside the X on the list of what is not allowed.

We are so careful now, taking shoes, socks
off as if on Holy Ground. The X ray portal,
gates to the heavens where minor sins

are scrutinized. A lighter for smokes, two
much make up, we have to come clean for
the frowning attendees. It is the air of

a routine stroll I notice as passengers
wheel contents like a trolley at the market,
be calm and carry on their motto. I miss

the sagging bags of last minute packs,
the leathery duffels to throw on a camel,
these plastic containers make everything

uniform like we are all business travelers,
not wanting to cause security distress if our
bag resembles the spasmodic stomach of

a fish eating too much plastic or worse
our bureau drawers at home. They must
be neat, tidy to go under the overhead's wing.

# Full

I bring the empty Tropicana
bottle now full of water to the tree
like an IV to keep it refreshed.

I pour the rest of it out.
Enough to keep a villager
alive in Kenya, the braided

stream an umbilical cord.
We collected the rain on
our roofs in Bermuda, kept

it in a tank with a palmetto
leaf spread open as any proud
peacock's tail to be so full.

# Every Civilization

Needs its pillars,
the rubber tree
is such in Coral Beach Club's domain.

Below, the roots pile like
dead bones from an excavation,
brown leaves archival paper

to pick up artifacts. I was
civilized here. The silver urn
for tea placed ritualistically on

the linen tablecloth as if
an altar. Liquid the colour
of elastic downpours into

an elephant's trunk in
an empire where all
human memory was stretched.

# England Taught Me

England taught me to love the rain,
the privacy it provides,
long tassled drops, on the Victorian
umbrella's edge of empire.

The splash of footsteps, waves made,
not allowed. There the quiet whispery
life, where even the sun must need
these rosaries strands of water for penance.

For being too bright, noticeable above,
creating the shadow grave of a person,
doing the ordinary. To remind them, hurry
up. Here is death's dark angel hovering.

# Memorial

The flags on the ground for each soldier,
in front of the town hall, eight inches at most,
fold over like birds landed, draped stripes, feathery.

Morning Classics is on my car radio and I try
to work out if Bach was influenced by Vivaldi?
Did Sebastian learn to escape his square-ness,

like the star spangled box with lines rushing light
into infinity? Notes in a score, crows on wires,
need the conductor's flutter of arms, wings.

The lost lives we honour today, with a hurried
picnic, folding chairs, popsicles melting, are ones
a coffin holds, and memory frees from de-composing

# Home Front

It appears that women in the 1920's
began to grow legs, ligaments evolved
from under moving skirts, just like

Darwin's notions. They tried to fly
as well, birds flapping around the dance
floor with realms of abundant feathers.

Husbands, fathers, boyfriends, brothers,
drop bombs the shape of lipsticks in WWII
where the explosion widens its mouth below

in enemy territory. While boundaries
shift, cave in at home, and women went to
work in pointy bullet bras to win another war.

# Wish Bone

It must be it has to do with flight,
bone the marrow to hold feathers
as Emily said of Hope. A wish must

fly, not be downward bound. When
one blows out candles, flames scurry,
yard birds take off. Wish bone,

two teethed comb, a woman pulls
out of the nest of hair, to cherub-wing
her face. Do we buy one when we

toss coins in an Italian fountain, let go
of Caesar's fare, as water streams, flutters
about to lift the volume of stone up?

# Ruling Bodies

Santa is placed on the porch,
cold, alone, a child put in a corner.
Physique not three dimensional,

rather sliced in half. A Jello
pudding of himself served on
a platter where his tummy jiggles.

Queen Victoria round, *morbidly
obese* as she said, swelled to become
a globe, as the British Empire

devours a world. Learned Urdu and
kept a journal, her script like waves
took her to the India she never saw.

Gandhi, a hanger with the spare cloth
of flesh, wore white like peace is a daily habit,
spun wool on a loom by the bare thrift of

shuttled patience. Walked the blank space
of his garb over multicolored India, became
an absence, present in such crowded quarters.

# Oration

Just when a president
returns to nationalism,
his country better, bigger,

the universe speaks,
wretches up seven new
planets in its mouth like

a Greek orator recites to
the sea, marbles under
his tongue. The world is

large, beyond borders,
beyond walls, the un-
known is the knowable.

Remember the US flag
on the moon, a cocktail
drink ornament on an olive.

# A Note

This is not the glassy truth I want
to be in front of. The computer's sheen,

cursor, the petite arrow, anthropologist's
tool to dig, chip at ice. Nor the keyboard

letters, alphabet blocks I can launch, hurl
into space like a child's nursery tantrum.

Email has its discreteness, slide a note
so quietly under another's door, but oh,

for the pen! It can row the tipped up
lines, waves of a sentence, like a slow oar.

My words are made of blood, flesh, pain,
joy and astonishment. I cannot place them

silently on a hospital white page, view
through a window, peer at an incubated baby.

# Because You Were Taught to Look

Because you were taught to look
and not to see, you raised the camera
to your eye, a protective mask
to grind the world down in one lens.

Because you were taught to look
and not to see, the paint brush
slowly lifted its torch of paint
into the cave of a canvas wall.

Because you were taught to look
and not to see, words shadow
the page, can only define
the space of light around them.

# Poldark

The hat Poldark wears looks
like a fortune cookie, dough
thumb printed to have three sides.

I would relish the telegram that
came out of the Chinese sweet,
like it was a mouth speaking.

A Giotto angel's lips pursed
in the halo of a plate as I sat
with a sixties boyfriend in a diner.

The future of the Cornish
sailers, miners, fishermen
in 1689 lay in the thin ribbon

of the sea, one could see at the edge
of the grassy cliffs. Likewise, I heard
calming rhythms on an island in

the Atlantic. The in, out tide chanting
my fate as the only one to be sure of,
an emptying and a replenishing.

# Not the Country I Was Born In

So no straight forward monotone,
just raised up high pitches, like a pinky
for tea, and then melting words,
breadfruit which couldn't survive heat,

sticky. A snapper flipping on a dock in
a pool of water, like a tongue
still full of the sea's rhythms
seeking an ocean's context.

A sentence as something to end?
Not so in the semi-tropics, enough
just to begin. In the U.K., a course
to jump your horse through for the

Queen. Not this U.S. banner for the self,
Chinese Cookie blurb about truest
you with lips pursed for a kiss.
This is not the country I was born in.

# Tide Tables

# Tide Tables

*for Art*

Each day I read the tide tables
in the Mid Ocean News. The graph
pitched like a sail in the right angle
of the square columns.  Overnight

a spider had spun a raggedy web
in a corner. I was always aware
of the high tide/low tide shift, as if
the island balanced itself on the tip

of a volcano. Low tide harbour,
high tide South Shore, high tide
harbour, low tide South Shore.
I read your in/out breathing

as it daily rose, fell, an inward
current, still here, still eager
for oxygen to infuse a body
with life. Your mouth gaped

open in an *o*, like a coin that
would drop into the splash
of your chest as it drew air in,
out. The oxygen machine puttering,

the sound of the ferry boat Georgia
idling at the Paget Dock, about to
resume its ride into Hamilton.
The last night of your breathing,

when I watched the crest of your
chest, rise, fall, when it told me
everything of how long you
would be lingering here, your

left lower rib so thin, as it went
up and down, the curve of your
bones pulling up flesh was a small
bird about to leave its nest, fly.

# Halter

I remove the oxygen tank
nose piece from your head,
hold a lasso of clear plastic
circles in my hand, remove

it like a halter over your hair.
You sit on your bed, pieces
of paper around as you write
as Matisse cut shapes in his

lasts days, piles all about him,
buried in work. The commode
with its pelican beak made us
laugh, ready to swallow any

debris, on its home environment
of a beach. Today in America
people watch an eclipse and
shout for joy when seen. Yours

I watch daily slivering you
thin, like the moon shadows
a sun. I adjust your fan, turn it
up, down, tuning a fine violin,

music only you hear. Whispery
sounds, the flapping of angel
wings, from a sole one,
to a band of them coming.

# Walker

His aluminum cane *clicks!*
*clicks!* as he walks the hall,
the sound of a camera shutter
closing on all the light, swallowing it.

The rod a pick like a paper one
used in parks, it punctuates silence
as it hits ground, collect seconds
of a life, keeping it tidy.

Soon one hand will become
two hands as he uses a walker,
like a gate before him which
bar will raise one day, open.

# Long Gaited

This is not a fast car, it is swift
like the Greek God Hermes,
wing-footed to out race clouds.
Sometimes it whistles while roving,

self-pleased with agility, the Jaguar
on the hood, a clothespin in
a nose, not to smell the ordinary.
To keep itself pure. When it fails

the CT emission test, the garage
attendant says the computer
can't translate reasons. I know
it is still full of the Devon air,

sea-full, curved by waves, like its
own *cresting* shape, crafted for speed
which makes a needle idle, falter:
a-metronome-attuned-to-long-gaited-spheres.

# Not Even Here

Not even here, where the cold ground
has a spread of snow, like white chips
from carving a marble tombstone.

Not even here do I want a dual act,
where we both spring out of the ground,
two slices of bread in a toaster. At

Manor Hovey last summer I reneged
sitting in chairs joined like Siamese
twins at the stomach, torsos bound.

Likewise, resisted riding a tandem
bicycle through Bermuda, the second
handlebar, a crooked Adam's rib. I

want to fly solo when the sky is
a swirl of movement, as headstone
becomes a surfboard to ride. Down

is up as stars fall back, sea unwraps
earth in crinkly tissue paper,
a crystal clear ball of predictions.

The cemetery full of jack in boxes
out-ed. Coffin lid a diving board,
I Jack Knife to cut a wake of blue.

# Jackets Hung

Without a body
in a row like
emptied selves,
buttons couldn't keep

inside. An army of
him in all weathers.
Sleeves like elephant
trunks full of memory's

blaring. The hanger's
steel crook above,
a question mark.
Where has he gone?

# Wag

*Do you want a bag?* The New Yorker
asks me at the lake where my dog
tries to defecate, haunches lowered
like a dump truck at the water's edge.
I say *No thank you!* Think body

bag, as my dog desists, coat brown
as the dirt's darkest granule,
the deep colour of dung. Oprah has
a guest who says our feces should
curl, like the tail of a dog as it swirls

the toilet. What is poetry that I can
write about such, and where a poem
becomes a village wag, eschews truth?
And holds the thump, thump of a dog's
last days, wags his whole life present.

# Heart Worm

The spiraling link to the red heart
worm tag, one about to wiggle
into it, as you did with mine.

The shape of inch worms
pulling themselves forward,
the shuffling moonwalk of

Michael Jackson. How nature
teaches us. The valentine
two wings like a child might

wear for a play, remind
everything no matter how
corporal red blooded will fly

away. I would pick up
a limestone rock on the island,
underneath slugs, like pursed lips,

centipedes with watchband
designs, spiders, knots clinging,
the underpinnings of a rug,

the threads that make a topical
woven design, like the absence
of your presence dangling.

# Bark

Rests head on my shoulder
as I drive the lake, like a ripe
mango settles on an island

stone wall. His muzzle is a boat
in the sea-wave map of Irish
Water Spaniel hair. We stop

for me to throw a stick
into the water he retrieves
water dripping on the sides,

an oversize Groucho Marx
mustache. At lunch he
still *whoofs* loudly for food,

bares frontal fangs *as* if
each bark was something
he can still sink teeth into.

# House Broken

*The house needs a dog!* I say
to Art. Stuart roamed one end
to the other, his motion
felt around us, like the stampeding
bison contained in the Lascaux cave.

Outside his circular tracks in
snow, dissolve in rain,
a lasso letting him go,
letting his memory become
ghostly. The downpour's

silver needles stitch up
the paw print holes he made
in the bright white, tracks of his earth
bound life as he went down to
the brook to drink. I took his collar

off, a few days before, unlocked
the leather and brass clasp as if
opening a gate to a field in Ireland
for him to roam: unclaimed, unnamed
as the unfettered puppy we once took in.

# Crackers

I look at the bandannas your groomer put
on you after each grooming. Triangular

like Tibetan prayer flags, they could be
tied together to blow in the wind. The shape

of the Bermuda triangle or of pyramids in
Egypt. Three sided as tissue party hats that

come out of British crackers, after pulling
handles shaped like crowns. The sound,

a one gun salute to you, to all we love. Life,
death tugs each end. What is the treasure

that spills out, the secret treat of such
torn friction, and celebratory party crack?

# Dogs with Tumours

Hangs on the chest,
a large tear, purse,
stitches leave a zipper,
mimics a jaw of teeth.

Has a gauze wrap
around a shin, makes
a fetlock, a thoroughbred
at the racetrack. Separates

his paw like a rabbit's
foot carried for luck.
Leaves blood from
trimmed claws, nail

polish streaks over
a clean kitchen floor.
Scratches a way out
of an antiseptic environ.

# Body Language

The technician asks me as he
holds the dark red vials with
my name on each one if they are
mine. I say *Yes!* The size, colour

of kindergarden crayons, I notice
tattoos on each of his muscled
biceps, a sense of vanity turns
them into Indian Temple columns.

The hands, legs and feet of Hindu
brides, laced with henna, cover
them like Eve's vine, a girlish
need for ornament, modest without

the needle's sting. The designs
on the technician's feather like,
his touch gentle as the nib enters
my arm. A pen in reverse draws

ink from my body into cartridges
full of the words I have not
written, cannot write yet from
my story, the body's own text.

# Map-Less

Google Earth alters terrains quicker than embassies,
like a jellyfish fluctuating in a tide, boundaries
on it recoil, increase before laws, deeds are
written out to guide. I use the street map icon,

compact human shape like a mini-shovel
to dig up memory, slide in and out of views
of Queen Street, Pomander Gate Road,
Hibiscus Lane, Kyber Pass. National Geographic

with a golden border, tinged by empires where
the sun never set. History framed in a gilded
moment worthy of museums. This world map-less,
like discovery is imminent every day. The familiar

shifts, so we don't know. The window view of
my neighbourhood, un-claimable, even through
the latitude, longitude of 12 x 12 panes, except as light
makes inky blots on the lawn in rubbed out mistakes.

# Jesus of the Highways

I understand why Catholics put Christ
on their dashboard. To have A friend who
puts his back to the winds, directs you
with traffic hand signals. Why the rearview

block of ice is adorned with the chains
of a rosary, to help a slippery back view be
negotiable. Side view mirrors flash light, stream,
give the car luminous wings, each journey

a mission. A French poet said *half vagrancy,*
*half pilgrimage.* The ride throws away land,
seeks a horizon, and a plastic Jesus moonwalks
a la Jackson, slip, slides all under his feet.

# Back Scrubber

Hangs from the shower,
bristles protrude earnest
as grass shoots on an April

lawn. Pink plastic holds
a mouth full of white
teeth. I play my torso

with it, a cellist with
a bow, it swings back
forth over my backside,

a horse's tail swishes,
eliminates flies. Parts of
my body, so hard to see

except in the oblong
vanity mirror's pool of
light, a tub from Bonnard.

I float on the glare, try to
swivel my head to locate,
see my back like my past

shimmers behind, ebbs me
quietly forward. The looking
glass gloss wing-like, shines.

# The Sun's Strobe

# Bone China

The shallow water in the vase, half an inch
at most at the bottom of green stems, ebbed,
sank down like nylon socks collapse on a calf.

*Pull up your socks!* Bravely said to one
another in daunting times. These sunflower
blooms have lived it to the end, sucked

all light from air with creased mouths,
bow out, each one to the space before
in this theatre of the round. I gather them:

a spindly bone corset, shaped to hold
a transparent center, in the middle of
a dining room where we eat off bone

china. Plates serve lunch prettily, daintily,
made from calcified animal skeletons,
once held a body together, collected it.

# Too Many Angels

Too many angels get on my nerves
as I decorate the wreath. They get,
got to fly in and out with their twitter
speech blurbs, the precursor of comics!

Give me the cows, udders pulled
them down into earth as calves sucked,
yank on their teats, children wanting
their toys. Mooing like moans,

horns on heads because they feel devilish.
And the camels too, the moving
mountains they are on a parched
journey where water sloshes inside.

No wonder the airs, the uppity pinched
face, hump a heap of wealth in such
sparseness. Down here below angels,
their profiles rise to a pitch, make waves.

# The Sun's Strobe

The four year old child in Florida wants to pick
up the snow, a toy she finds for the first
time. Yes, it makes a pink flamingo sparkle

like a sugar coated cookie. Standing outside
the Plaza in my teens was when I first saw sleet.
More the blinding flash of the sun' strobe

collecting the moment within dark shadow.
The height of skyscrapers notch the long
descent down, nature so far away. Here,

a blizzard hangs windows with the staunch
peace of Victorian veils. Shawls put on
mirrors when someone is deceased. To

look at oneself alone in reflective light,
too glaring a task, while outside the hollow
becomes luminous, shimmers with negative space.

# Sealed Silence

Like the sun is cold too,
marbled by the snow, wall
eyed in a descending madness,
can only cast shadows of white

everywhere like a film negative.
The postman says: *Stay warm!*
Brings mail to the door, my first
cell phone arrives, beams no service.

What is felled in such downward
movement of ice? Frequencies
interrupted? I clasp it shut, a mouth
tight as an oyster, wait for a word

to become a pearl. How can I
write if I don't know such
sealed silence? Have its currents
form, polish what is held deep within.

# Liposuction

A kind of liposuction of sorts,
men on the side of the clapboard
white colonial with layers of pink
insulation foaming, surgeons remove fat.

Or, stuffing it around the cold bones
of pipes to create a body of warmth.
The substance, tissuey as cotton candy
served at the Green Fair in August. My

upstairs pipes freeze as if punishment
for not letting the faucets babble, I
rarely go up to turn on. Now they emit
only a silence. How close to the elements

we live, albeit heat shakes out of old
radiators like flour from an iron sifter.
Somedays to make it to the postbox is its
own feat, footsteps frozen from the day

before as if to encourage. Envelopes with
hospital corners keep mail warm. Snug. How
letters melt the heart, imagine the writing hand
rising up, down, like a swimmer in the tide of a line.

# First Christmas Card

So fitting my first Christmas card
comes from a trash man, drags
the large garbage bag towards
the dumpster, engine reeves,
steams, a snorting beast.

Santa away with my rubbish,
what to discard in this season
of giving, do without.
His three Magi card,
surely will hit the heap.

Cigarette in hand like a pencil
an elf writes down my
Christmas list with. The smoke
curls around his chin
into a Paste on St. Nick's Beard.

The Wise Men on the greeting
look up at the stars to seek
an unfound treasure in heaven.
I empty trash weekly into a plastic
lined can, dark as any black hole.

# Wreath

Surprised by how large it is,
it comes in three sections,
each one curved into the puffy
breast of a shot pheasant.

The joiners steel mouths
arced like the goat skin flasks
shepherds drank from. Such bounty.
I put it in front of my hearth,

the spiral of Celtic green,
a mothering circle. Round as
a belly button, a mouth, a nipple.
I could not adorn a tree this year

where a Christmas bulb might fall,
break. The Times Square Ball.
Reminds me as ornaments bounced
in the waves of boughs how

fragile each year is. I prefer
this rotund roundness, camels,
and angels alike ride a carousel
which merrily blurs all endings.

# Relief

Like the trees would rather have not
gotten out of bed this morning. They
are half dressed, stand as if in a doorway
with piles of dead leaves at their feet,
days of uncollected mail on the porch.

They had quite a party through late
October, dressed for fun, to shine in
the dark when a car headlights made them stars.
They burnt themselves out performing in front
of so many fans, strangers. They deserve

the moment to not be noticed. No one gazes
at them now, but look straight ahead as they
drive by. They must be relieved to think
Christmas trees will now have the attention,
the burden of cheering the masses placed elsewhere.

# Dead Head

Dead heading day lilies,
I think of braindead rock
stars of the sixties of which
this is not unalike. The sense

that too much brightness
blasted through, so heads
hang, dejected mops, careful
to clean up the sky from

all traces of a currency. I
pick them off, hold, like
a ladies glove, worn to
church to worship the sun.

Like the wee robin I held
in my hand late spring, all
flight gone from the fan
of wings, brown as fins

of a Bermuda Grunt, brown
with the wriggling of earth,
the dark crawl of worms,
a hook curved to catch it.

Bud, a golden digit to count
days by, the chopped off
finger of an Old Testament
thief for stealing the light.

# Fistfuls

The piece of maple wood
the Tompkins spliced, sharp
as an ax in the fire, scalps

the flames' wavy hair. A bead
bright barrette holds strands
of light, in night's dark

mane. Like a blond going
grey, the smoke rushes up
the chimney in fistfuls.

# How to End Winter

Take your black parka to the cleaners,
firstly winter took you there,
bankrupted you. The jacket, a puffy
body bag, a suitable mattress to
lie the stiff months on. Then

never pick it up so it becomes
an orphan, lined up, hopeful
among furs bristling like bears,
the thin strapped dresses with
the hanger's elbows poking out.

Next year you will decide to buy
a new one, and so will take it to
the thrift shop where it will do
its winter thieving for someone else,
absorbing heat, light's seasoned burglar.

# Clean Up

It is all about cleaning up, the large
shovels on the town truck slam into
the bank while its light twirls the 12
x 12 panes around my dining room,
angels dancing, as if they came inside

to clean me up too. I need them as I
turn the fireplace into a stable in my
mind, grate with wood, a manger, fire
the light of the child. A real clean it all
up act. If this isn't working for you

then let's leave it with the windows
reflecting in the room like molars.
I'm in the jaws of winter, the steely
mouth on the truck eats snow, a hungry
dinosaur before Christmas was ever born.

# Day After Valentines

The large red New England
barn peels, cracks like
the leather cover
of an old classic.

Inside, stacked hay,
pages of a bound book
stained with dust,
sealed for so long, drifts, fritters.

The moon has read
the contents with her
dangling monocle all
night long. The farm's

wooden gate rests between
the old stone walls,
the harp she left.
It is propped open.

# Spring Rising

The forsythia curving itself in
arcs on the cusp of the small hill
reminds me with buds every few inches

of prayer beads Muslims rotate in
hands on pilgrimages through deserts
to mosques hooked to quarter moons.

The epitome of a fast, of the not full
container to which chanting always
aspires. The forsythia notched like

Nedra's hair pulled into braids at Holy
Tabernacle Church with clips every
few inches. Praise required a harnessing

of energy into reins to pull on. Her head
a spider of sorts, beautiful in insect-ness.
how the mind can wander aimlessly,

scurry into corners. The branches of
the forsythia buds, bees swelling
in flight after being disturbed bring

spring's honeyed light. A sunrise
near in the corner which is not rising,
spreading limbs across the sky

to fly away, but here until I
too can rise, bow over, rise, lift
hands, arms up, arc, sway into spring.

# April Fools

The forsythia branches
curve with the clash of
swords as spring fights
winter back like pirates
fought over a bobbing ship's
domain in a clamourous sea.

Bent in the arc of a twiggy bow,
the bush shoots out sparks of
buds to win back a season.
The singed cusp of Icarus's wing,
we now all yearn to fly too close
to the sun, even if we perish by fire.

# About the Author

Nancy Anne Miller is a Bermudian poet with seven books: *Somersault* (*Guernica Editions* CA 2015), *Because There Was No Sea* (Anaphora Literary Press USA 2014), *Immigrant's Autumn* (Aldrich Press USA 2014 ). *Water Logged* (Aldrich Press 2016), Star Map (FutureCycle press 2016), *Island Bound Mail* (Kelsay Books 2017) Boiling Hot ( Kelsay Books 2018). Her poems have appeared *in Edinburgh Review (UK), Agenda (UK),Ambit (UK), Stand (UK),The International Literary Quarterly (UK), Magma (UK), Journal of Postcolonial Writing (UK),Wasafiri(UK), Mslexia (UK), New Welsh Review (UK), The Moth (IE),A New Ulster (IE), Southword Journal (IE), Poetshead (IE), Poetry Ireland Review (IE), Dodging the Rain (IE),The Fiddlehead (CA), The Dalhousie Review (CA),The Toronto Quarterly blog (CA), Postcolonial Text (CA), Transnational Literatures (AU),The Caribbean Writer (VI), tongues of the ocean (BS),Sargasso: Journal of Caribbean Literature (PR), Bim (BB), Poui (BB), Moko: Caribbean Arts and Letters (TT),Commentaries(FM), The Arts Journal (GY) sx salon: (CAR), The Pacuare Anthology (CR), Metaphor (PH), The Missing Slate (PK), The Open Road Review (IN), Papercuts (IN),The Taj Mahal Review(IN), Poetry Salzburg Review (AT), BM Publishers (ZA),Proud Flesh: New Afrikan Journal of Culture, Politics, Consciousness (USA), Journal of Caribbean Literatures (USA), St. Katherine's Review (USA), Hampton Sydney Poetry Review(USA), Theodate (USA), Free Verse: A Journal of Contemporary Poetry and Poetics* (USA), *Interviewing the Caribbean* (USA), among others. She has an MLitt in Creative Writing from Univ. of Glasgow, is a MacDowell Fellow, and is a three time recipient of Bermuda Art Council Grants. She teaches poetry workshops in Bermuda, and represented Bermuda in Poetry World Cup. She organized Ber-Mused, a poetry reading for BDA's 400th in 2009. She was shortlisted for the small axe salon (Caribbean) poetry prize (2013), guest edited *tongues of the ocean (BS),* and was included in *Arts Etc Barbados* (BB) tribute for Edward Kamau Brathwaite.

Kelsay Books

www.ingramcontent.com/pod-product-compliance
Lightning Source LLC
Chambersburg PA
CBHW030958090426
42737CB00007B/585